D1037329

+<=[A Math]~±÷

Journey Around the WONDERS OF THE WORLD

Hilary Koll & Steve Mills

Crabtree Publishing Company
www.crabtreebooks.com

Crabtree Publishing Company
www.crabtreebooks.com
1-800-387-7650

Published in Canada
616 Welland Ave.
St. Catharines, ON
L2M 5V6

Published in the United States
PMB 59051, 350 Fifth Ave.
59th Floor,
New York, NY

Published in 2016 by CRABTREE PUBLISHING COMPANY.
All rights reserved. No part of this publication may be reproduced, stored in a retrieval system or be transmitted in any form or by any means, electronic, mechanical, photocopying, recording, or otherwise, without the prior written permission of the copyright owner.

First published in 2015 by Wayland
(A division of Hachette Children's Books)
Copyright © Wayland 2015

Authors: Hilary Koll and Steve Mills
Commissioning editor: Elizabeth Brent
Editors: Joe Fullman, Rob Colson, Kathy Middleton and Janine Deschenes
Proofreader: Petrice Custance
Math Consultant: Diane Dakers
Designer: Ed Simkins
Prepress technician: Katherine Berti
Print and production coordinator: Katherine Berti

Production coordinated by Tall Tree Ltd

Photographs:
iStockphoto: 4-5 Ugurhan Betin, 6 turtix, 7tr ConradFries, 7br paulprescott72, 9 bestphoto, 10–11 bjdlzx, 12–13 BartZuidema, 12l OliverChilds, 12r sinopics, 13b OliverChilds, 14–15 RodReis, 16–17 heckepics, 19t Emmanouil Filippou, 19b Lingbeek, 20 kjorgen, 22–23 isoft, 24–25 charmedesign, 26t MindStorm-inc, 26cl benjamint444, 26cr shalamov, 27, 31 tlindne. All other images by Shutterstock.

The website addresses (URLs) included in this book were valid at the time of going to press. However, it is possible that contents or addresses may have changed since the publication of this book. No responsibility for any such changes can be accepted by either the author or the Publisher.

Printed in Canada/022016/IH20151223

Library and Archives Canada Cataloguing in Publication

Koll, Hilary, author
A math journey around the wonders of the world / Hilary Koll, Steve Mills.

(Go figure!)
Includes index.
Issued in print and electronic formats.
ISBN 978-0-7787-2321-9 (bound).--
ISBN 978-0-7787-2329-5 (paperback).--
ISBN 978-1-4271-7719-3 (html)

1. Mathematics--Juvenile literature. 2. Seven Wonders of the World--Juvenile literature. I. Mills, Steve, author II. Title.

QA40.5.K64 2016 j510 C2015-907941-1
C2015-907942-X

Library of Congress Cataloging-in-Publication Data

Names: Koll, Hilary, author. | Mills, Steve, 1955- author.
Title: A math journey around the wonders of the world / Hilary Koll and Steve Mills.
Description: New York, NY : Crabtree Publishing, 2016. | ©2015 | Series: Go figure! | Includes index.
Identifiers: LCCN 2015049849 (print) | LCCN 2016001344 (ebook)
ISBN 9780778723219 (reinforced library binding : alk. paper)
ISBN 9780778723295 (pbk. : alk. paper)
ISBN 9781427177193 (electronic HTML)
Subjects: LCSH: Mathematics--Juvenile literature. | Historic sites--Juvenile literature.
Classification: LCC QA40.5 .K65 2016 (print) | LCC QA40.5 (ebook) | DDC 510--dc23
LC record available at http://lccn.loc.gov/2015049849

go figure!

Get ready for the trip of a lifetime as you use your mathematical skills to collect information for a travel guide to the wonders of the world.

CONTENTS

04 THE PYRAMIDS OF EGYPT

06 THE TAJ MAHAL

08 WATERFALLS OF THE WORLD

10 THE GREAT WALL OF CHINA

12 THE TERRACOTTA ARMY

14 THE AMAZON

16 ANTARCTICA

18 THE ACROPOLIS

20 BURJ KHALIFA

22 MOUNT EVEREST

24 STONEHENGE

26 GALÁPAGOS

28 GO FIGURE! ANSWERS

30 MATH GLOSSARY

32 LEARNING MORE AND INDEX

Words in **bold** appear in the glossary on pages 30–31.

Answers to the Go Figure! challenges can be found on page 28.

Please note: The standard and metric systems are used interchangeably throughout this book.

WHAT EQUIPMENT DO YOU NEED?

Pen or pencil

Notepad

You might find some of the questions in this book are too hard to do without the help of a calculator. Ask your teacher about when and how to use a calculator.

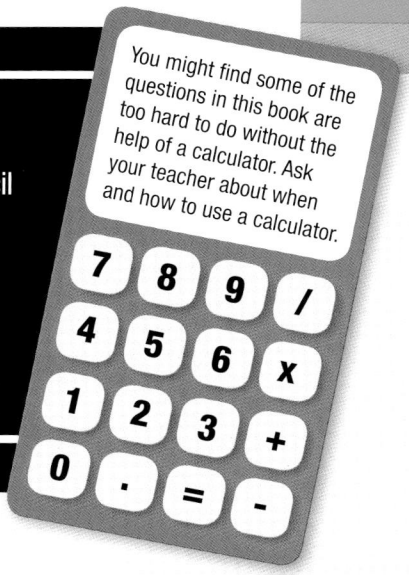

MISSION 1

THE PYRAMIDS OF EGYPT

Your first mission takes you to Egypt. Three giant stone pyramids were built there more than 3,000 years ago as burial tombs for Egyptian kings. They still tower above the desert sands. Your task is to figure out their sizes.

LEARN ABOUT IT

PYRAMIDS, NETS, AND SURFACE AREAS

A pyramid **is a 3-D shape with a base and triangular faces. A square-based pyramid has a square base and four triangular faces. The top point of the pyramid is called its apex.**

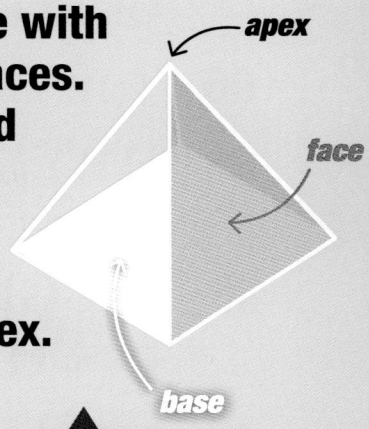

A net is a flat pattern that is folded to make a 3-D shape. The net of a square-based pyramid has four triangles (the faces) and a square (the base) joined together. They can be joined in different ways. One example is shown at right:

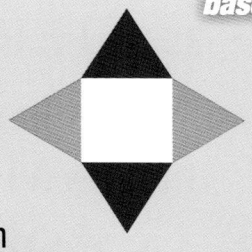

You can find the **area** of a rectangle by multiplying its length by its width. So, to find the area of a square, multiply the length by itself. To find the area of a triangle, multiply the length of the base (shown as b) by the perpendicular height (shown as h) and divide the answer in half. This can be shown as the formula:

area of a triangle = ½b × h

To find the **surface area** of a pyramid, find the area of each part of the net and add them together.

›GO FIGURE!

You need to find out the measurements of the pyramids so that you can add the information to your travel guide. The tallest pyramid is called the Great Pyramid and was built for Pharaoh Khufu, the second-tallest was built for Pharaoh Khafre, and the shortest was built for Pharaoh Menkaure.

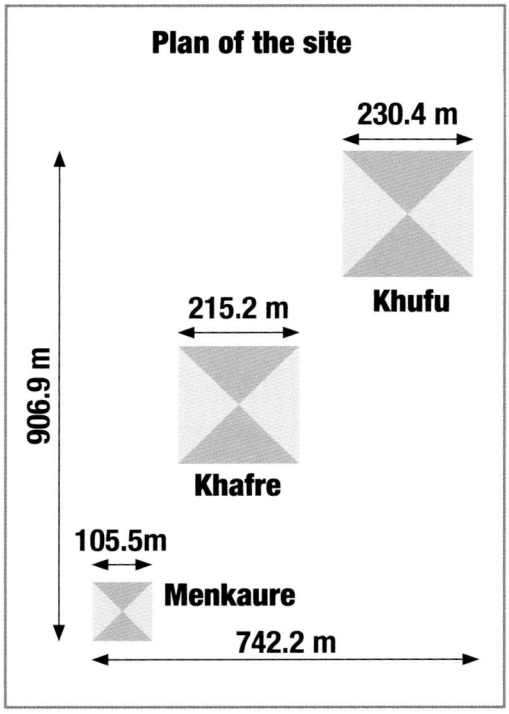

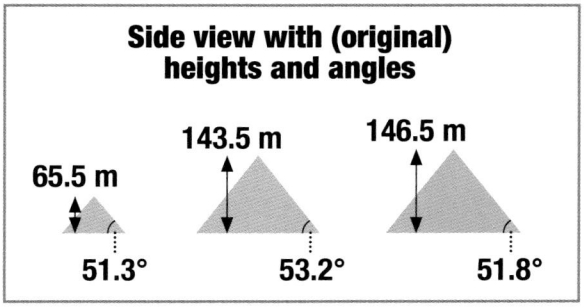

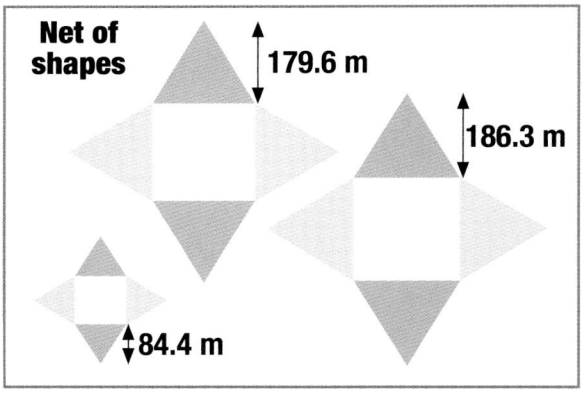

1. For each pyramid, find the area of the square base.
2. Due to erosion, the height of Khufu's pyramid (the Great Pyramid) has decreased since it was built. It is now 7.7 m shorter. What is its current height?
3. Using the original heights shown above, how much taller was the second-tallest pyramid than the shortest pyramid?
4. For each of the pyramids, use the nets to find the surface area of the whole 3-D shape.

MISSION 2

THE TAJ MAHAL

Your next mission takes you to India to report on the Taj Mahal, a beautiful burial structure that includes a reflecting pool.

LEARN ABOUT IT

TRANSFORMATIONS AND SYMMETRY

Transformations **are ways of moving geometric shapes. They include reflection, rotation, and translation. These three transformations do not change the size or angles of the shapes.**

Reflections are made when shapes are flipped over a line, showing what they would look like in a mirror.

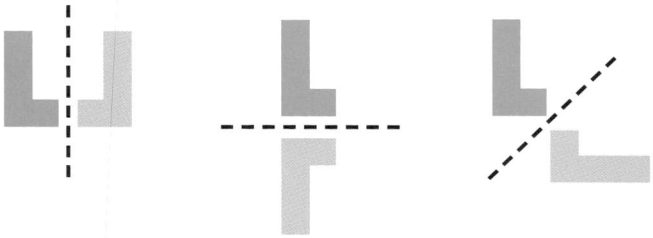

Rotations are made when shapes are turned around a center point. They can be turned by different amounts and in different directions.

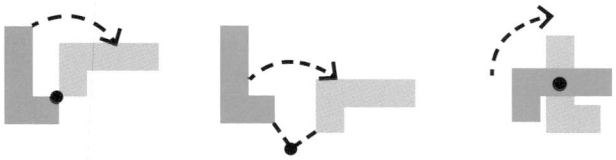

The examples above show a quarter, or 90°, turn to the right.

Translations are made when you slide a shape without turning or reflecting it. You can slide a shape horizontally, vertically, or diagonally.

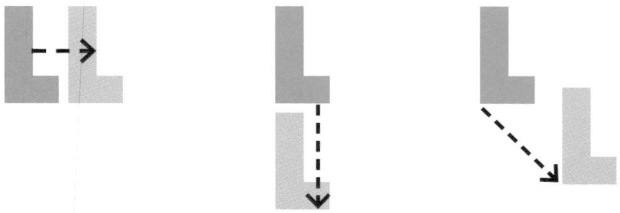

Symmetry is when a shape or object has parts that make it look the same when the shape is reflected or rotated.

- Reflection symmetry is when one half of the shape is the reflection of the other half. A **line of symmetry** is any folding line across the shape that makes the sides of the shape meet up exactly.
- Rotational symmetry is when the shape looks the same after being turned. The number of times it can be turned and look the same before it is upright again is called the order.

Shape	Number of lines of reflection symmetry	Order of rotational symmetry
L	0	1
♥	1	1
⬟	5	5

›GO FIGURE!

For this section of the travel guide, you need to describe the amazing patterns, symmetries, and geometric shapes found in the Taj Mahal. Study the photos below that you took.

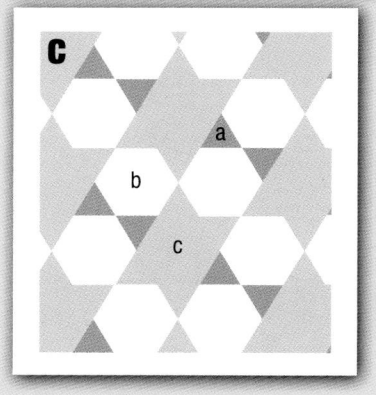

1. How many lines of reflection symmetry does photo A show?
2. How many full translations are shown in the repeating pattern in photo B?
3. Photo C shows a tile pattern made from three different shapes: a) equilateral triangles (3 equal sides), b) regular hexagons (6 sides & 6 lines of symmetry), and c) another shape. What is shape c?
4. In total, how many lines of symmetry do each of the shapes a, b, and c have?
5. Photo D shows lawns shaped like the polygon drawn below. Describe the shape by its number of sides, as well as its number of lines of reflection and rotational symmetry. How many right angles (90°) does it have? How many other kinds of angles?

MISSION 3

WATERFALLS OF THE WORLD

You want to include one of the world's major waterfalls in your guide, but you can't decide which one. So, you'll need to gather lots of information and compare the data.

LEARN ABOUT IT
COMPARING AND ROUNDING NUMBERS

When comparing and rounding numbers, it is important to know the values of the digits, or individual numbers.

To put numbers in order from largest to smallest, line up the digits in the correct columns and compare them from left to right, as shown below. If two digits in a column are the same, compare the digits to their right, and so on.

Ten thousands	Thousands	Hundreds	Tens	Ones
4	2	6	9	2
4	2	3	5	7
3	9	9	0	4
	9	9	8	6

Rounding to the nearest 10
If the digit in the Ones column is 5 or more, the Tens digit goes up by one, and the Ones digit becomes zero. If the Ones digit is less than 5, the Tens digit stays as it is, and the Ones digit still becomes zero.

Rounding to the nearest 100
If the digit in the Tens column is 5 or more, the Hundreds digit goes up by one. The digits in the Tens and Ones both become zero. If the Tens digit is less than 5, the Hundreds digit stays as it is. The digits in the Tens and Ones become zero.

Rounding to the nearest 1,000
If the Hundreds digit is 5 or more, the Thousands digit goes up by one. The digits in the Hundreds, Tens, and Ones become zero. If the Hundreds is less than 5, the Thousands digit stays as it is, and the digits in the Hundreds, Tens, and Ones become zero.

Number	Rounded to the nearest 10	Rounded to the nearest 100	Rounded to the nearest 1000
5,829	5,830	5,800	6,000
23,687	23,690	23,700	24,000
18,009	18,010	18,000	18,000

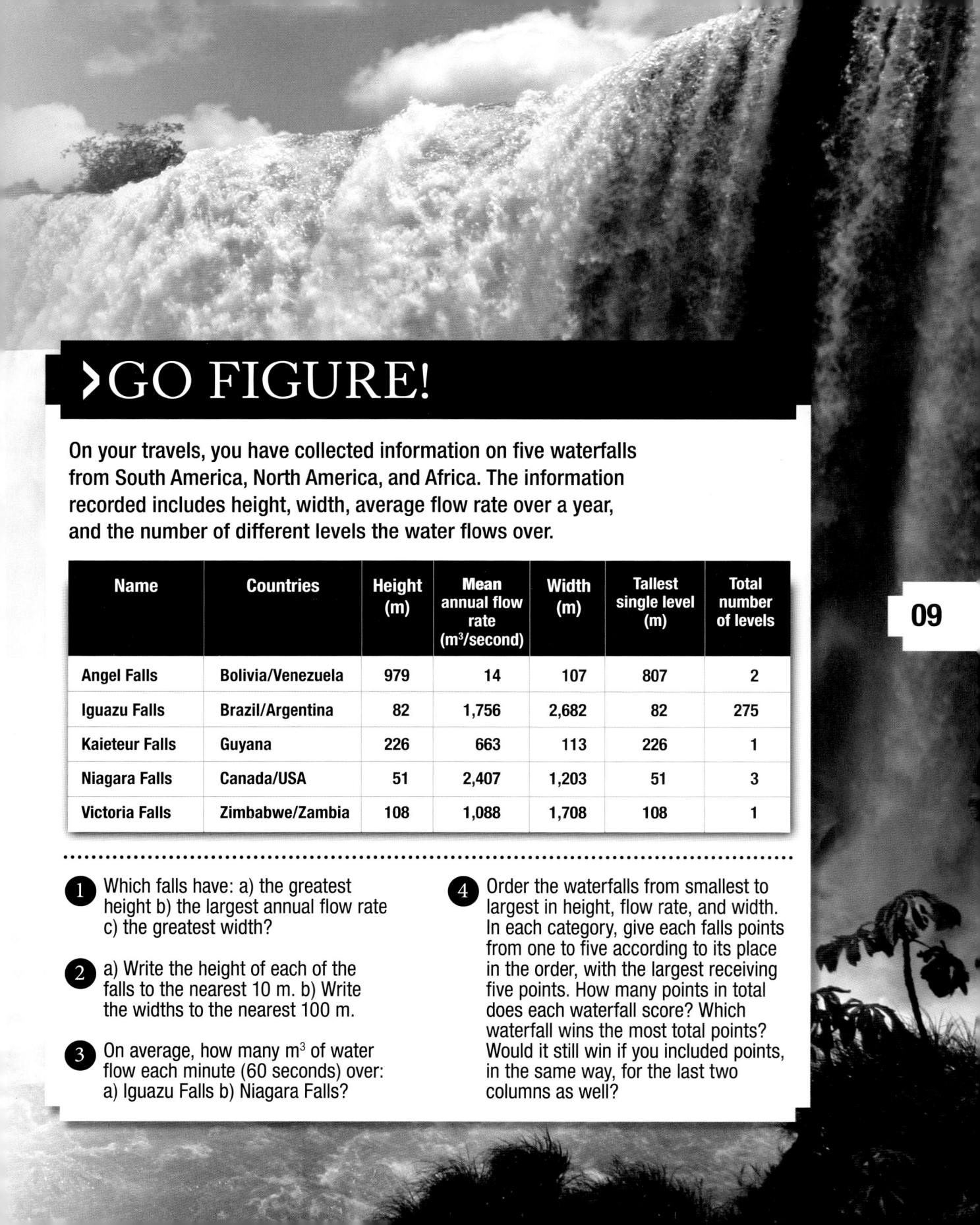

›GO FIGURE!

On your travels, you have collected information on five waterfalls from South America, North America, and Africa. The information recorded includes height, width, average flow rate over a year, and the number of different levels the water flows over.

Name	Countries	Height (m)	Mean annual flow rate (m^3/second)	Width (m)	Tallest single level (m)	Total number of levels
Angel Falls	Bolivia/Venezuela	979	14	107	807	2
Iguazu Falls	Brazil/Argentina	82	1,756	2,682	82	275
Kaieteur Falls	Guyana	226	663	113	226	1
Niagara Falls	Canada/USA	51	2,407	1,203	51	3
Victoria Falls	Zimbabwe/Zambia	108	1,088	1,708	108	1

1. Which falls have: a) the greatest height b) the largest annual flow rate c) the greatest width?

2. a) Write the height of each of the falls to the nearest 10 m. b) Write the widths to the nearest 100 m.

3. On average, how many m^3 of water flow each minute (60 seconds) over: a) Iguazu Falls b) Niagara Falls?

4. Order the waterfalls from smallest to largest in height, flow rate, and width. In each category, give each falls points from one to five according to its place in the order, with the largest receiving five points. How many points in total does each waterfall score? Which waterfall wins the most total points? Would it still win if you included points, in the same way, for the last two columns as well?

MISSION 4

THE GREAT WALL OF CHINA

To visit the next two wonders of the world, you must travel to China. Here you'll find the Great Wall of China, a structure thousands of miles long, built hundreds of years ago to keep invaders out of the country.

LEARN ABOUT IT LARGE NUMBERS

When describing large numbers, we group digits in threes from right to left. Groups of three are usually separated by a comma, as in the example: 473,695.

O	Ones
T	Tens
H	Hundreds
Th	Thousands
TTh	Ten thousands
HTh	Hundred thousands
M	Millions
TM	Ten millions
HM	Hundred millions
B	Billions
TB	Ten billions
HB	Hundred billions

In 26,789, the 26 stands for how many thousands are in the number. Written out, it is twenty-six thousand seven hundred eighty-nine.

Thousands			Ones		
HTh	TTh	Th	H	T	O
	2	6	7	8	9

In 55,031,044, the 55 stands for how many **millions**, and the 031 stands for how many thousands. Written out, it is fifty-five million thirty-one thousand forty-four.

Millions			Thousands			Ones		
HM	TM	M	HTh	TTh	Th	H	T	O
	5	5	0	3	1	0	4	4

In 2,104,030,001, the 2 stands for how many **billions**, the 104 stands for how many millions, and the 030 stands for how many thousands. Written out, it is two billion one hundred four million thirty thousand one.

Billions			Millions			Thousands			Ones		
HB	TB	B	HM	TM	M	HTh	TTh	Th	H	T	O
		2	1	0	4	0	3	0	0	0	1

Numbers can also be described in thousands, millions, or billions, like this:

5,000,000	= **5 million**
5,600,000	= **5.6 million**
800,000	= **800 thousand or 0.8 million**
400,000,000	= **400 million or 0.4 billion**
1,300,000,000	= **1.3 billion**

›GO FIGURE!

For your travel guide, you must provide information on the size of the Great Wall, as well as facts and figures relating to the numbers of tourists.

1. Write in words: a) the official length of the Great Wall, b) the circumference of the equator, c) the **estimated** total length of the different branches that make up the wall.

2. Using numbers and a decimal, write in millions the number of visitors to China from overseas in: a) 2014, b) 2013, c) 2012.

3. Using the estimate for the number of visitors to the Great Wall each year, estimate the total number of visitors to the Great Wall over 10 years. Give your answer: a) in words, b) in numbers, c) in millions with a decimal, d) in billions with a decimal.

The official length of the Great Wall is 8850 km, made up of 6259 km sections of wall, 359 km of trenches, and 2232 km of natural barriers such as hills and rivers. The walls are around 8 m wide and range from 5 m to 8 m tall.

Including all the different branches of the Great Wall, it is estimated to be 21,196 km long, which is more than half the distance around the equator (the **circumference** of the equator is 40,075 km).

This table shows the number of tourists coming from overseas to China in recent years.

Year	Number of overseas visitors
2014	26,360,800
2013	26,290,300
2012	27,191,600

The Great Wall alone receives an estimated 10.72 million visitors each year.

MISSION 5

THE TERRACOTTA ARMY

While in China, you can visit the amazing Terracotta Army. Eight thousand life-size statues of warriors and their horses standing in rows were uncovered in the ancient tomb of China's first emperor. Made of clay called terracotta, every statue has its own expression.

LEARN ABOUT IT

LONG MULTIPLICATION, AREA, SHORT DIVISION

To do long multiplication, or multiplying by a number that is two digits or more, you need to know short multiplication (mulitiplying by one number).

You also need to know how to multiply by a multiple of 10. To do this, put a zero in the Ones column and multiply by the Tens digit.

```
    1 2
     746
×      4
  ------
    2984
```

short multiplication

```
    1 2
     746
×     40
  ------
   29840
```

multiplying by a multiple of 10

In long multiplication, you multiply the top number by the Ones digit, then by the multiple of 10, and add the two answers together. Here are a couple of examples:

```
      1
      3
     251
×     36
  ------
    1506   251 × 6
+   7530   251 × 30
  ------
    9036
```

```
      5 2
      2 1
     984
×     73
  ------
   2952   984 × 3
+ 68880   984 × 70
  ------
  71832
```

The example to the right shows how to divide 84,690 by 6, using short division. Working from left to right, 6 can go into 8 one time with 2 remaining. The two joins with the next number, 4, to become 24. Continuing, 6 can go into 24 four times with zero remaining, then 6 goes into 6 one time, and so on.

```
     14115
    2   3
6 | 84690
```

›GO FIGURE!

Report on the number of terracotta soldiers and the area of each burial vault, or chamber, for your travel guide. Area is found by multiplying length by width. The result is expressed in meters squared, or m^2.

Excavation of more than 1500 statues is still going on.

Excavation of 68 figures, four horses, and a wooden chariot.

Vault 2
Crossbowmen, charioteers, and cavalry
Size of vault: 94 m x 84 m

Vault 3
Officers
Size of vault: 21 m x 17 m

Vault 1
Main army (infantry)
Size of vault: 210 m x 62 m

One quarter of the area has been excavated, revealing more than 1500 statues (out of an estimated 6000).

1. In Vault 1, the three front rows each have 68 soldiers. How many soldiers in total are in these rows? Use short multiplication.
2. There are also 9 trenches in vault 1. Each trench has 36 rows of four soldiers. Use short multiplication to find out the total number of soldiers.
3. Use long multiplication to find the area, in m^2, of: a) Vault 3, b) Vault 2, c) Vault 1.
4. Only one quarter of Vault 1 has been excavated. Use short division to figure out the area of the excavated part of Vault 1.

MISSION 6

THE AMAZON

Your next mission takes you to Brazil in South America, to the mighty Amazon River and rain forest. Packed with wildlife, the huge rain forest covers a larger area than the rest of the world's rain forests put together.

LEARN ABOUT IT

HECTARES AND MULTIPLYING BY 100

Areas of land are often measured in hectares**. One hectare is equal to 10,000 m², which is the area of a square measuring 100 m by 100 m.**

A full-sized soccer field is a bit smaller than one hectare.

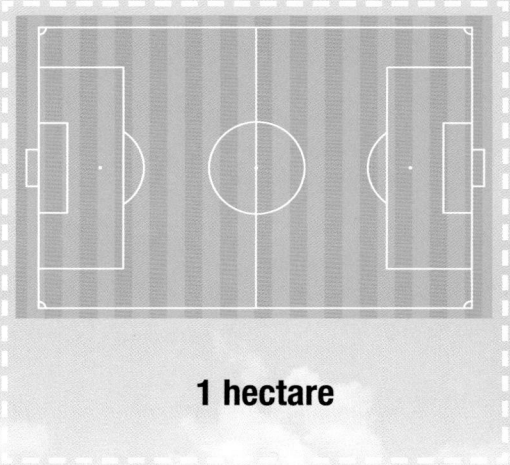

1 hectare

The area of a square that is 1 km x 1 km is 1 km². This is equal to 100 hectares. In other words, 1 km² = 100 hectares.

To multiply a number by 100, move the digits of the number two places to the left and add two zeros in the Tens and Ones columns.

Millions			Thousands			Ones			
HM	TM	M	HTh	TTh	Th	H	T	O	
		5	5	0	0	0	0	0	5,500,000
5	5	0	0	0	0	0	0	0	×100
		1	2	2	5	8	0	0	1,225,800
1	2	2	5	8	0	0	0	0	×100

The area of the Amazon rain forest is 5.5 million km^2. In the example on the bottom of the previous page, this number is multiplied by 100 to determine how many hectares the area is. Similarly, the other example shows that an area of 1,225,600 km^2 = 122,560,000 hectares which is 122.56 million hectares.

5,500,000 km^2 = 550,000,000 hectares, which can also be written as 550 million hectares.

›GO FIGURE!

The rain forest is under constant threat of deforestation by loggers and farmers. You must report on how much of the rain forest has been deforested and whether the rate has increased or decreased.

The table shows the average number of km^2 of Amazon rain forest destroyed in Brazil between 1988 and 2014.

Period of time (9 year periods)	1988–1996	1997–2005	2006–2014
Average area of land deforested per year	17,400 km^2	19,400 km^2	8,600 km^2

1. From 1988–1996, how many km^2 of land was destroyed in total over the 9 year period?
2. How much more land was deforested each year during the 1997–2005 period than in 1988–1996 period? Give your answer in hectares.
3. How much less land was deforested each year during the 2006–2014 period than in 1997–2005 period? Give your answer in hectares and also as the number of million hectares.
4. Calculate the total amount of land deforested from 1988 to 2014. Give your answer as the number of million hectares.

MISSION 7

ANTARCTICA

The next part of your journey takes you on a cruise past the towering icebergs of Antarctica, the coldest place on Earth. Due to its extreme temperatures, tourists visit only in the area's summer months between November and March.

LEARN ABOUT IT

NEGATIVE NUMBERS AND TEMPERATURE

Temperature uses both positive **and** negative numbers. **Negative numbers below zero degrees Celcius (0°C) —the freezing point— are colder. Positive numbers above 0°C, bring warmer weather.**

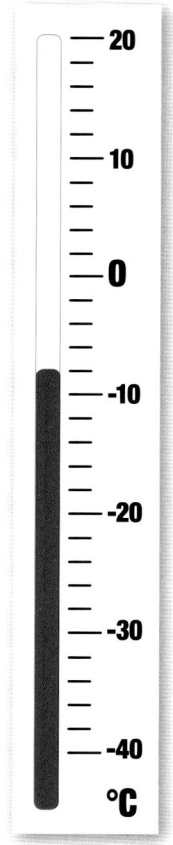

The thermometer on the right reads -8°C (minus eight degrees Celsius). Since water freezes at 0°C, that means it could snow.

To find how much colder one temperature is than another, count down from the warmer temperature to the colder temperature.

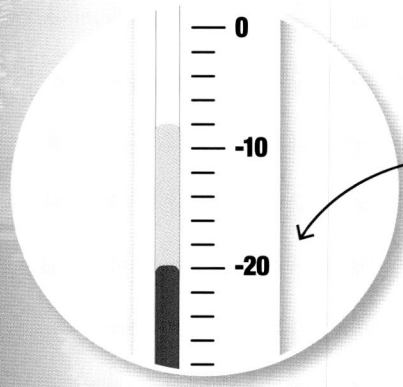

-20°C is 12 degrees colder than -8°C.

›GO FIGURE!

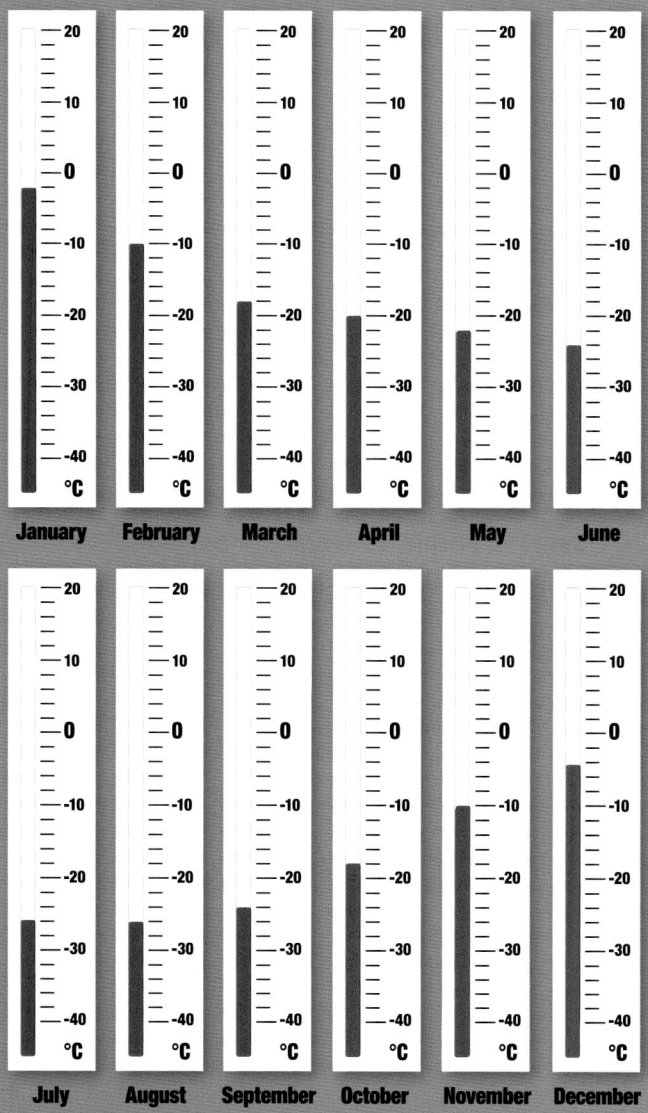

Find out about expected temperatures at different times of the year to provide information for your travel guide. These thermometers show the **mean** average temperatures in each month at one location on the coast of Antarctica.

1. Find the mean average temperature (to 1 decimal place) over the three summer months by adding the readings in December, January, and February, and dividing the total by 3.
2. How much warmer is the warmest month in the year than the coldest month?
3. How much colder is it in: a) September than in February? b) March than in November?
4. Find the mean average temperature over the whole year by adding all readings and dividing by the total number of months.

MISSION 8

THE ACROPOLIS

In Athens, Greece, you must gather information on the dimensions of the Parthenon—the ruins of a famous temple that was part of an ancient settlement high on a hill, called the Acropolis.

LEARN ABOUT IT

GOLDEN RATIO AND GOLDEN RECTANGLES

Mathematicians discovered a special number that occurs in nature, art, and geometry. They called it phi**. The mathematical symbol for phi is φ.**

The value of phi is approximately 1.6180339887498948482045868 34… (The … means the entire number carries on longer than is shown here.)

Phi is a key part of a **ratio** known as the golden ratio. The golden ratio is written as 1:φ (or 1:1.618…). It can best be seen in a rectangle whose width represents 1, and whose length is 1.618… times greater than its width.

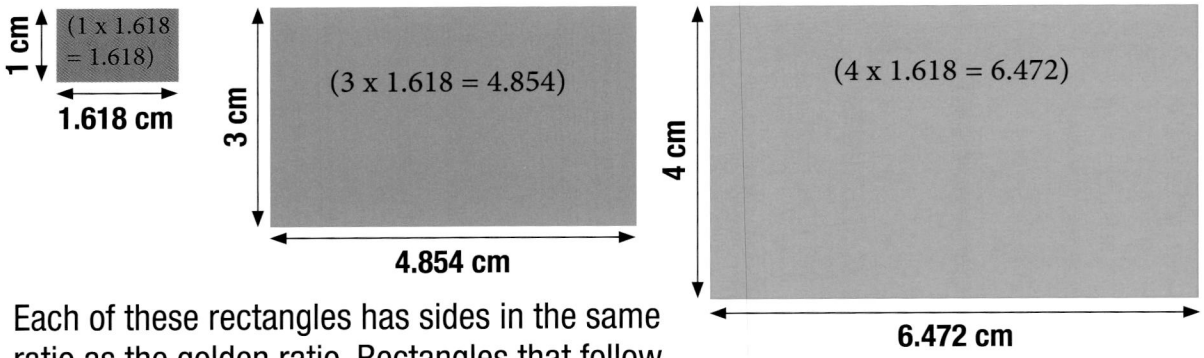

Each of these rectangles has sides in the same ratio as the golden ratio. Rectangles that follow the golden ratio are called golden rectangles. If you draw a line to make a square inside a golden rectangle, the rectangle that is left over is also a golden rectangle. In the example below, if you draw an arc from corner to corner in repeated golden rectangles, it forms a spiral pattern that is often seen in art, architecture, and nature.

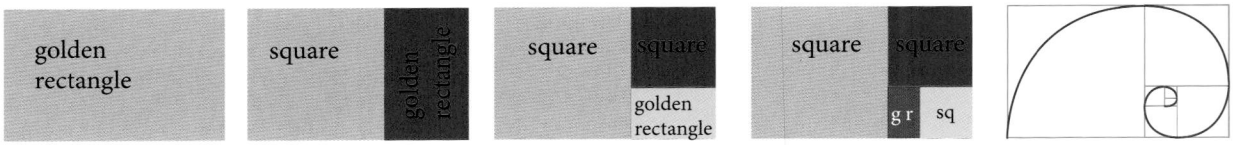

›GO FIGURE!

You measure the length of the base of the rectangle at the front of the Parthenon and find that it is 30 meters across. You learn that, although the roof of the ruin is now flat, it used to come to a point at the top.

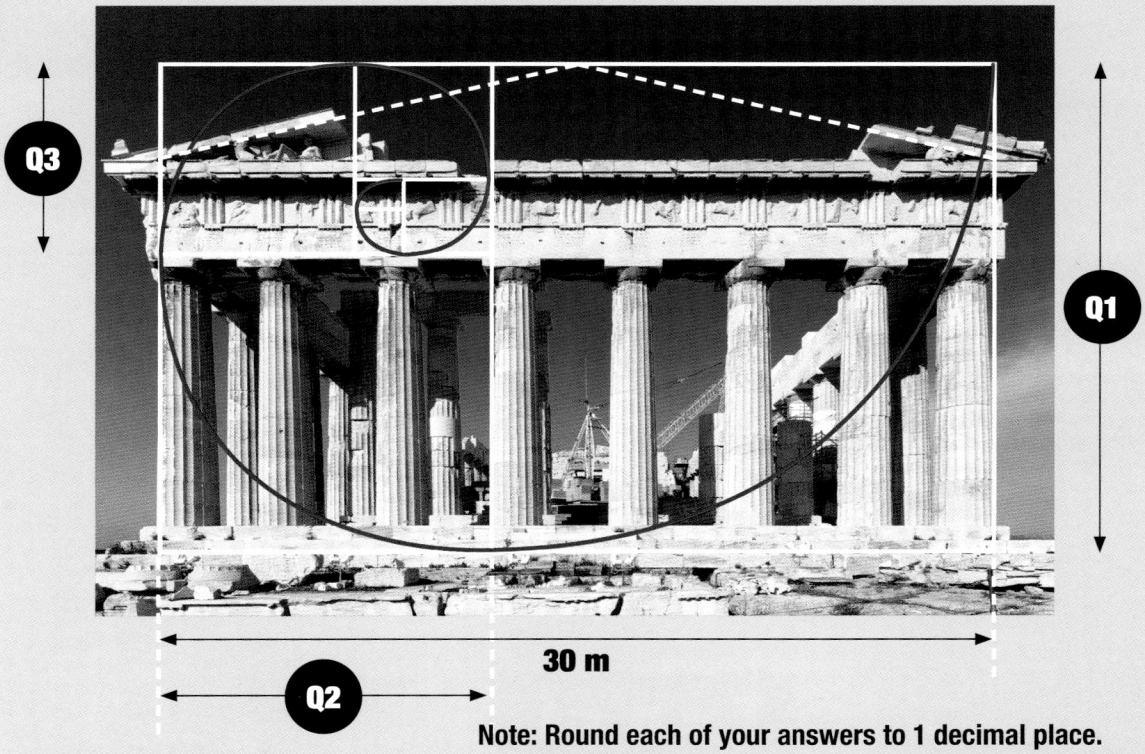

Note: Round each of your answers to 1 decimal place.

1. Use a calculator to figure out an approximate height of the roof, from the base of the building to its original point, by dividing 30 m by the number φ (using φ rounded to 1.618).

2. Draw a golden rectangle around the Parthenon. Draw a line to create a square on the right inside the rectangle, then a square to its left. Divide your answer to question 1 by φ to find the pillars' height.

3. Divide your answer to question 2 by φ to find the distance from the top of the pillars to the top of the original roof.

MISSION 9

BURJ KHALIFA

The world's largest skyscraper, the Burj Khalifa, towers above the city of Dubai in the United Arab Emirates. You can use **algebra** to uncover some fascinating facts about it.

LEARN ABOUT IT
ALGEBRA AND FORMULAE

Algebra is a branch of math that uses formulas to show relationships between things. The formulas use letters or symbols to stand in for different things.

For example, let's find the total length of water pipe needed for a skyscraper. The letter "T" will stand in for the answer, "Total length of pipe required." The letter "n" will stand in for the "number of floors" the skyscraper will have. The letter "l" will stand in for the "length of pipe needed for each floor." So the mathematical formula is:

$$T = n \times l$$

The builders know "n" is 20 floors and "l" is 615 m of pipe per floor. We can find the total length of pipe needed by substituting these two numbers into the formula:

$$T = 20 \times 615$$
$$T = 12{,}300 \text{ m}$$

How long will it take to get to the top of this tower? The formula below calculates "t," the time an elevator takes to travel a distance, by dividing "d," the distance, by "s," the elevator's speed.

$$t = d \div s \quad \text{or} \quad t = d / s$$

Using the formula at the bottom of the previous page, we can figure out the time it would take an elevator to go a distance of 78 m traveling at a speed of 6 meters per second.

$t = 78 \div 6$
$t = 13$ seconds

This algebraic formula converts temperatures given in degrees Fahrenheit (°F) to degrees Celsius (°C).

$\frac{5}{9}(F - 32) = C$

›GO FIGURE!

You are told some of the facts about the Burj Khalifa. Use this information in the formulas to find out more.

The Burj Khalifa in Dubai is 828 m tall.

It has 163 floors that contain offices and 1044 residential apartments.

The outside temperature at the top of the tower is 68°F on the day you arrive.

The floor area is 309,473 m².

There are 57 elevators, and the main service elevator rises 504 m.

The outside of the building is covered with 28,261 glass panels.

The Burj Khalifa's water system supplies an average of 946,000 liters per day.

1. Using the formula $T = n \times l$, find the total length of water pipe used in the Burj Khalifa (using $l = 615$ m). Give your answer first in meters and then in kilometers.

2. Use the formula $t = d \div s$ to find how long it would take to travel up 504 m in the elevator, moving at an average speed of:
a) 6 m/s, and b) 8 m/s
Give your answers in seconds and minutes.

3. What is the temperature at the top in degrees Celsius (°C) on the day you arrive?

MISSION 10

MOUNT EVEREST

The highest wonder, Mount Everest, soars above Nepal and Tibet, about 8,850 m above sea level. Climb to the top, using fractions and **percentages** to plan your mission.

LEARN ABOUT IT
FRACTIONS AND PERCENTAGES

Parts of a whole can be written as fractions. In a fraction, the number representing the whole is on the bottom and is called the denominator. The number representing a part is on the top and is called the numerator.

For example, your goal is to climb 8,000 m, almost to the very top of Everest. The first day you climb part of the way, up to 2,000 m. This can be written as the fraction shown at right:

$$\frac{2{,}000}{8{,}000}$$

Fractions can often be written in a simplified form. Both top and bottom numbers may be reduced by dividing each one by a **factor** they have in common. A factor is one of the numbers that are multiplied together to create the top or bottom numbers. In this example, the largest factor that can go into both 2,000 and 8,000 evenly is 2,000. Dividing each number evenly by the largest factor makes this fraction ¼. It still holds the same value as $^{2{,}000}/_{8{,}000}$, but it is easier to work with.

$$\frac{2{,}000}{8{,}000} \overset{\div 2{,}000}{\underset{\div 2{,}000}{=}} \frac{1}{4}$$

Sometimes, when numbers are very large, it is easier to divide several times to reach the simplest form.

$$\frac{3{,}540}{8{,}850} \overset{\div 10}{\underset{\div 10}{=}} \frac{354}{885} \overset{\div 3}{\underset{\div 3}{=}} \frac{118}{295} \overset{\div 59}{\underset{\div 59}{=}} \frac{2}{5}$$

Fractions can also be expressed as percentages. To write a fraction as a percentage, divide the numerator by the denominator. Then, multiply your answer by 100. This is the fraction written as a percentage.

Here are some examples:

$$\frac{1}{4} = 1 \div 4 \times 100 = 25\%$$

$$\frac{11}{20} = 11 \div 20 \times 100$$

It is useful to learn the percentage equivalents of one third and two thirds also:

$$\frac{1}{3} = 33.33\% \qquad \frac{2}{3} = 66.67\%$$

›GO FIGURE!

At various points up Mount Everest, there are base camps that provide safe places to rest on your journey to the summit. You'll need to give information in your guide about what proportion of the way up these and other points of interest are.

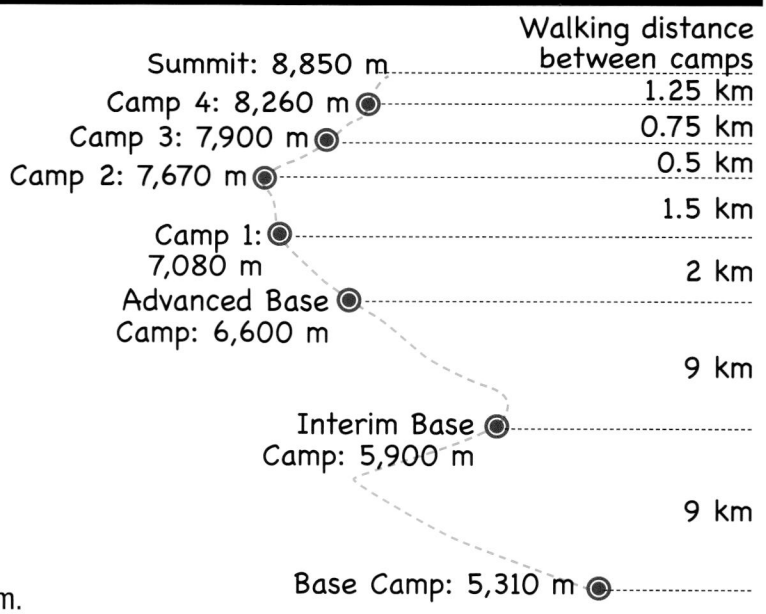

Give your answers to these questions in their simplest form.

1. What fraction of the Summit height of Everest is:
   a) Base Camp, b) Interim Base Camp, c) Camp 1, d) Camp 2, e) Camp 4?

2. Write each of these as a percentage of the Summit height of Everest:
   a) Base Camp, b) Interim Base Camp, c) Camp 1, d) Camp 2?

3. The walk from Base Camp to the Summit is 24 km in total. What fraction of this distance is the walk from:
   a) Base Camp to Interim Base Camp?
   b) Advanced Base Camp to Camp 1?
   c) Camp 1 to the Summit?
   d) Advanced Base Camp to the Summit?

4. What fraction of the entire walk is the walk from Advanced Base Camp to the Summit? What is it as a percentage?

MISSION 11

STONEHENGE

The prehistoric monument of Stonehenge, in England, is made up of giant stones standing in circles. For your mission, measure them and include their dimensions in your guide.

LEARN ABOUT IT
CIRCLES AND MEASUREMENTS

The radius **of a circle is the distance from the edge to its center. It is half the size of the** diameter**, which is the widest distance across the circle, through the center.**

The circumference is the distance all the way around the outside of the circle. It is another word for the **perimeter** of the circle.

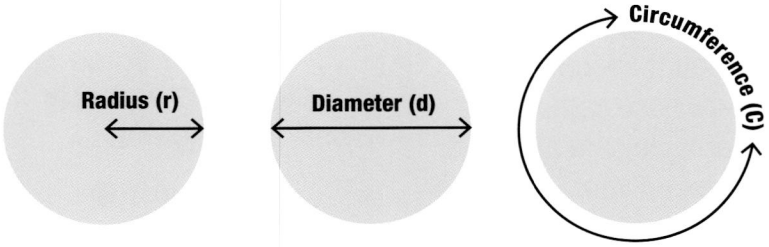

There is a special relationship between the diameter (d) of a circle and its circumference (C). For every circle, the circumference will always be 3.1412… times the diameter. (The … means the number goes on longer than is shown here.) We call this number **pi**. The mathematical symbol for pi is π. Pi is a never-ending number, so it is usually rounded to 3.14 when calculating formulas.

The formula for circumference can be written as $C = \pi \times d$. Because the radius is half the diameter, the formula can also be written as $C = \pi \times 2 \times r$. Formulas are often written without the multiplication signs as:

$$C = \pi d$$

and

$$C = 2\pi r$$

To find the area of a circle, use the formula Area = $\pi \times \text{radius}^2$.
When you multiply something by itself, we say it is squared.
The short form of the formula can also be written as:

$$A = \pi r^2$$

›GO FIGURE!

At Stonehenge, you learn about the different circles making up the ancient monument, as shown on this diagram. The table below gives the approximate radius of each circle.

Circle Name	radius
Outer Chalk Bank	56 m
Inner Chalk Bank	45.5 m
Aubrey Circle of Holes	44 m
Circle of "Y" Holes	27.5 m
Circle of "Z" Holes	20 m
Exterior of the Sarsen Circle	16.5 m
Interior of the Sarsen Circle	15.4 m
Outer Bluestone Circle	12.1 m
Great Trilithon Horseshoe	7.7 m
Inner Bluestones Horseshoe	6 m

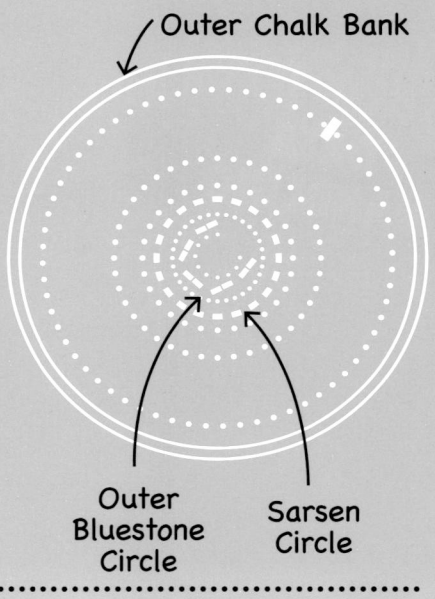

Round all your answers to 1 decimal place.

1. Find the diameter of the: a) Outer Chalk Bank, b) Exterior of the Sarsen Circle, c) Interior of the Sarsen Circle, d) Outer Bluestone Circle.

2. Using pi rounded to 3.14, use your answers from question 1 to figure out the circumference of:
a) Outer Chalk Bank
b) Exterior of the Sarsen Circle
c) Interior of the Sarsen Circle
d) Outer Bluestone Circle.

3. Use a calculator to find the approximate area of the Interior of the Sarsen Circle.

MISSION 12

GALÁPAGOS

Your final mission takes you to the wondrous Galápagos Islands, off the coast of South America. The islands are home to many rare and magnificent animals.

LEARN ABOUT IT
DATA HANDLING

When reading tables, make sure you read the row and column headings carefully.

This table shows information on **population** changes to some of the animals of the Galápagos. Over the centuries, their numbers have decreased because of tourism, hunting, and the introduction of animals not native to the islands, such as rats, cats, and dogs. Some of the island's animals have no defenses against these newcomers. Since 1970, a breeding program has restored some of the numbers.

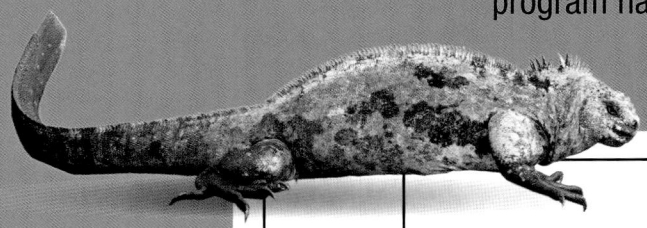

	Estimated populations of:			
Year	**Blue-footed boobies**	**Iguanas**	**Tortoises**	**Sea lions**
1600	unknown	unknown	**250,000**	unknown
1830	unknown	unknown	**150,000**	**80,000**
1900	unknown	**10,000**	**50,000**	**50,000**
1970	**20,000**	**1,000**	**6,000**	**40,000**
2014	**6,400**	**9,000**	**25,000**	**10,000**

On this **line graph**, you can figure out the measure of each space between the unnumbered gray lines on the vertical **axis** by dividing the first number on the axis (5,000) by the number of lines from 0 to 5,000 (5 lines). So each line is worth 5,000 ÷ 5, or 1,000. To find the population in a particular year, follow the dotted line up from the year to the red line, then go left along the gray line at that point to the number on the vertical axis. To find when the population was a particular size, read across from that population number until you reach the red line. Then read down to the year.

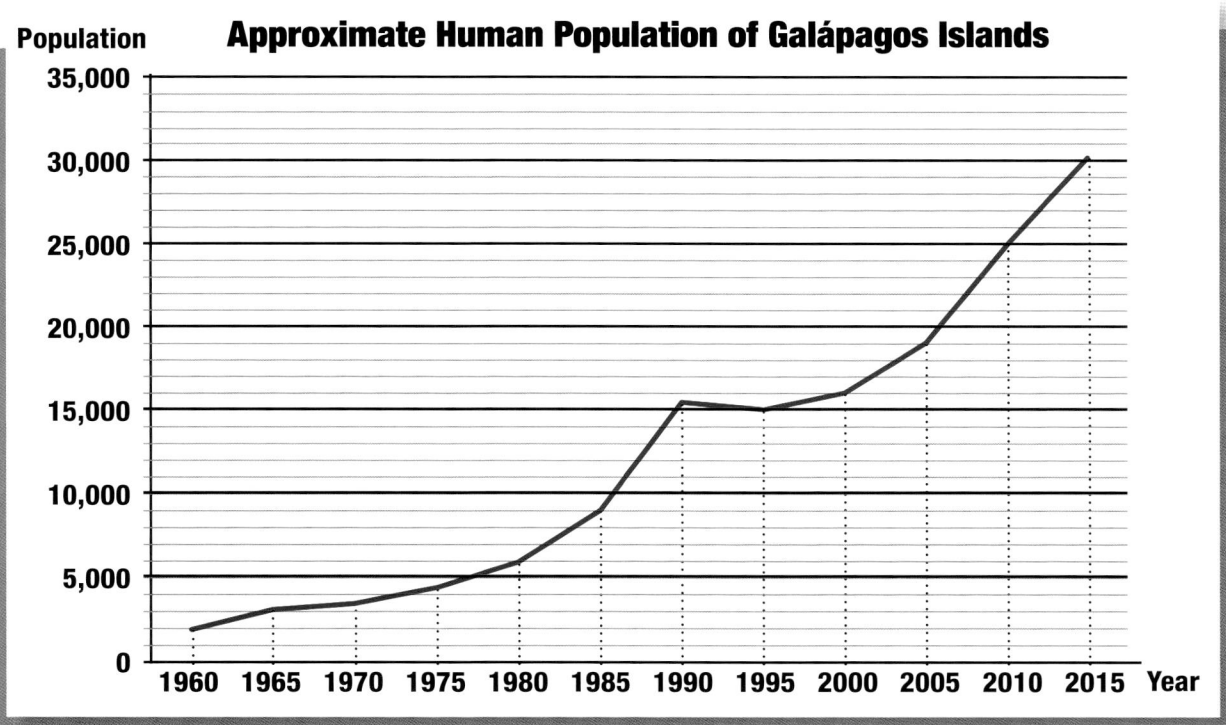

›GO FIGURE!

Interpret the graphs and tables to find facts and stats to include in your travel guide.

1. Due to whalers killing tortoises for food, the population of tortoises declined greatly between 1830 and 1900. By how many did it decline?
2. In what year did the human population reach 25,000?
3. Sea lion numbers are strongly affected by El Niño (a weather system with warm waters). By how many did their population decline between 1970 and 2014?
4. Approximately how much greater is the human population in 2015 than it was in 1970?

GO FIGURE! ANSWERS

04–05 The Pyramids of Egypt

1. 230.4 x 230.4 = 53,084.16 m^2
   215.2 x 215.2 = 46,311.04 m^2
   105.5 x 1.05.5 = 11,130.25 m^2
2. 146.5 – 7.7 = 138.8 m
3. 143.5 – 65.5 = 78 m
4. (½ x 230.4 x 186.3) x 4 + 53,084.16
   = 138,931.2 m^2
   (½ x 215.2 x 179.6) x 4 + 46,311.04
   = 123,610.88 m^2
   (½ x 105.5 x 84.4) x 4 + 11,130.25
   = 28,938.65 m^2

06–07 The Taj Mahal

1. Photo A shows two lines of reflective symmetry.
2. There are two full translations in the pattern.
3. Shape c is also a hexagon.
4. a has three? lines of symmetry
   b has six? lines of symmetry
   c has two? lines of symmetry
5. The shape has:
   16 sides,
   16 lines of reflective symmetry,
   A rotational symmetry order of 16,
   8 right angles,
   8 obtuse angles.

08–09 Waterfalls of the World

1. a) Angel Falls has the greatest height.
   b) Niagara Falls has the largest flow rate.
   c) Iguazu Falls has the greatest width.
2. a) Angel Falls – 980 m
   Iguazu Falls – 80 m
   Kaieteur Falls – 230 m
   Niagara Falls – 50 m
   Victoria Falls – 110 m
   b) Angel Falls – 100 m
   Iguazu Falls – 2700 m
   Kaieteur Falls – 100 m
   Niagara Falls – 1200 m
   Victoria Falls – 1700 m
3. a) 105,360 m^3 b) 144,420 m^3
4. Iguazu Falls scores the most points with 11, and it would still score the highest if the last two columns were included, with 18 points.

10–11 The Great Wall of China

1. a) Eight thousand, eight hundred fifty kilometers
   b) Forty thousand, seventy-five kilometers
   c) Twenty-one thousand, one hundred ninety-six kilometers
2. a) 26.3608 million
   b) 26.2903 million
   c) 27.1916 million
3. a) One hundred seven million, two hundred thousand
   b) 107,200,000
   c) 107.2 million
   d) 0.1072 billion

12–13 Terracotta Army

1. 3 x 68 = 204 soldiers
2. 9 x 36 x 4 = 1296 soldiers
3. a) 21 x 17 = 357 m^2
   b) 94 x 84 = 7896 m^2
   c) 210 x 62 = 13,020 m^2
4. 13,020 ÷ 4 = 3255 m^2

14–15 The Amazon

1. 17,400 x 9 = 156,600 km^2
2. 19,400 – 17,400 = 2000 km^2
   = 200,000 hectares
3. 19,400 – 8600 = 10,800 km^2
   = 1,080,000 hectares
   and 1.08 million hectares
4. (17,400 x 9) + (19,400 x 9) + (8600 x 9)
   = 408,600 km^2 = 40.86 million hectares

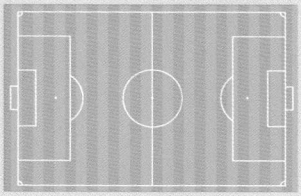

16–17 Antarctica

1. Mean temperature in summer:
   (December + January + February)/3
   (-4 + -2 + -10)/3 = -5.3°C
2. January (-2) 24 degrees warmer than July and August (-26). i.e. (-2- -26) = 24.
3. a) September is 14°C colder than February.
   b) March is 8°C colder than November.
4. The mean average temperature for whole year is: -2 + -10 + -18 + -20 + -22 + -24 + -26 + -26 + -24 + -18 + -10 + -4
   = -204 ÷ 12 = -17°C

18–19 The Acropolis

1. 30 divided by φ is approximately 18.5 m
2. 18.5 divided by φ is approximately 11.4 m
3. 11.4 divided by φ is approximately 7.1 m

20–21 Burj Khalifa

1. 163 x 615 = 100,245 m or 100.245 km
2. a) 504 ÷ 6 = 84 seconds
   or 1 minute 24 seconds
   b) 504 ÷ 8 = 63 seconds
   or 1 minute 3 seconds
3. $\frac{5}{9}$ (68 – 32) = 20°C

22–23 Mount Everest

1. a) 5310/8850 = $\frac{3}{5}$
   b) 5900/8850 = $\frac{2}{3}$
   c) 7080/8850 = $\frac{4}{5}$
   d) 7670/8850 = $\frac{13}{15}$
   e) 8260/8850 = $\frac{14}{15}$
2. a) 60% b) 66.7% c) 80%
   d) 86.7% e) 93.3%
3. a) $\frac{9}{24} = \frac{3}{8}$, b) $\frac{2}{24} = \frac{1}{12}$
   c) $\frac{4}{24} = \frac{1}{6}$, d) $\frac{6}{24} = \frac{1}{4}$
4. $\frac{6}{24} = \frac{1}{4}$ = 25%

24–25 Stonehenge

1. a) Outer Chalk Bank
   diameter = 56 x 2 = 112 m
   b) Exterior of the Sarsen Circle
   diameter = 16.5 x 2 = 33 m
   c) Interior of the Sarsen Circle
   diameter = 15.4 x 2 = 30.8 m
   d) Outer Bluestone Circle
   diameter = 12.1 x 2 = 24.2 m
2. a) 112 x 3.14 = 351.7 m
   b) 33 x 3.14 = 103.6 m
   c) 30.8 x 3.14 = 96.7 m
   d) 24.2 x 3.14 = 76.0 m
3. 3.14 x 15.4 x 15.4 = 744.7 m^2

26–27 Galápagos

1. 150,000 – 50,000 = 100,000
2. 2010
3. 40,000 – 10,000 = 30,000
4. 30,000 – 3500 = 26,500

MATH GLOSSARY

ALGEBRA
A type of mathematics that replaces numbers in equations with letters

AREA
The amount of two-dimensional space covered by a shape or object. For example, the area of a rectangle is calculated by multiplying the length of one of the short sides by the length of one of the long sides.

AXIS
A line that is used in math to locate a point

BILLION
A thousand million

CIRCUMFERENCE
The perimeter of a circle, which is the distance all the way around the edge

DIAMETER
The widest length across a circle, passing through the center

ESTIMATE
To produce an answer that is roughly equivalent to the correct answer. Estimating usually involves rounding the numbers involved up or down.

FACTOR
A number that multiplies with another number to make a third number

HECTARE
An area of 10,000 m^2

LINE GRAPH
A type of graph that shows a sequence of data, connecting the values with a continuous line.

LINE OF SYMMETRY
A mirror line that divides a shape into two reflected halves. The lines marked are all lines of symmetry.

MEAN
A type of average that is calculated by adding together a collection of figures and then dividing by the number of figures. The mean of the numbers 2, 3, and 4 is: $(2 + 3 + 4) \div 3 = 3$.

MILLION
A thousand thousand

NEGATIVE NUMBER
A number that is less than zero

PERCENTAGE
A percentage shows one number as a fraction of another number, given in hundredths. Each percentage point represents $1/100$ of the total.

PERIMETER
The total distance around a shape. The perimeter is calculated by adding together the lengths of all the shape's sides.

PI
Written as π, pi is a special number that is approximately 3.1412… or 22/7. It is the relationship between the diameter and circumference of a circle.

PHI
Written as φ, phi is approximately 1.618... and can be written exactly using the formula $\frac{1+\sqrt{5}}{2}$.

POPULATION
The number of people, or animals, that live in a particular area, such as a town, region, or country

POSITIVE NUMBER
A number that is greater than zero

PYRAMID
A three-dimensional shape whose sides are formed from triangles that meet at a point above a polygon base. The base can be a triangle, square, rectangle, or any shape with three or more sides.

RADIUS
The distance between the center of a circle and its circumference

RATIO
Ratios show how one or more numbers or values is related to another. So a ratio of 2:1 shows that there are twice as many of the first value as there are of the second.

ROUNDING
Changing a number up or down to the nearest ten, hundred, or thousand. For example, 11 can be rounded down to 10, while 18 can be rounded up to 20.

SURFACE AREA
The sum of all the areas of all the shapes that cover the surface of an object

SYMMETRY
When a shape or object has parts that are the same when they are reflected or rotated

TRANSFORMATIONS
These are ways of changing or moving a shape. There are four main types of transformations: reflection, rotation, translation, and enlargement.

LEARNING MORE

WEBSITES

www.mathisfun.com
A huge website packed full of explanations, examples, games, puzzles, activities, worksheets and teacher resources for all age levels.

www.khanacademy.org
A website for all ages that contains practice exercises and easy-to-follow instructional videos on all subjects including math.

www.mathplayground.com
An action-packed website with maths games, mathematical word problems, worksheets, puzzles and videos.

INDEX

algebra 20–21
apex 4
area 4–5, 14–15

Celsius 16, 21
circles 24–25
circumference 24–25
comparing numbers 8–9

diameter 24–25
division 13

Fahrenheit 21
formulas 20–21
fractions 22–23

geometry 18–19
golden ratio 18–19
golden rectangle 18–19

hectare 14

line graph 27

multiplication 12, 14

negative numbers 16–17
net 4–5

percentages 22–23
phi 18–19
pi 24–25
pyramid 4–5

radius 24–25
rectangle 4, 18
reflection 6
rotation 6
rounding 8

simplifying 22
symmetry 7

tables 15, 26–27
temperature 16–17
thermometers 16–17
transformations 6–7
translation 6
triangles 4–5